United States Presidents

Warren G. Harding

Paul Joseph
ABDO Publishing Company

visit us at
www.abdopub.com

Published by ABDO Publishing Company, 4940 Viking Drive, Edina, Minnesota 55435.
Copyright © 1999 by Abdo Consulting Group, Inc. International copyrights reserved in
all countries. No part of this book may be reproduced in any form without written
permission from the publisher.

Published 1999
Printed in the United States of America
Second printing 2002

Cover and Interior Photo credits: AP/Wide World, Corbis-Bettmann

Contributing editors: Robert Italia, Tamara L. Britton, K. M. Brielmaier
Book design/maps: Patrick Laurel

Library of Congress Cataloging-in-Publication Data

Joseph, Paul, 1970-
    Warren G. Harding / by Paul Joseph.
       p. cm. -- (United States presidents) (Checkerboard president series)
    Includes index.
    Summary: A simple biography of the popular senator from Ohio who
was elected as twenty-ninth president of the United States in 1920.
       ISBN 1-57765-234-7
       1. Harding, Warren G. (Warren Gamaliel), 1865-1923--Juvenile
literature. 2. Presidents--United States--Biography--Juvenile
literature. [1. Harding, Warren G. (Warren Gamaliel), 1865-1923.
2. Presidents.] I. Title. II. Series III. Series: United States
presidents (Edina, Minn.)
E786.J76 1999
973.91'4'092--dc21
    [B]   98-13896
                                                                  CIP
                                                                  AC

Contents

Warren G. Harding

*I*n 1920, Warren G. Harding was elected the twenty-ninth president of the United States. He won the election by more than seven million votes.

World War I ended just before the 1920 election. Many Americans were out of work and had little money. Harding promised to return the country to a simpler, easier time.

President Harding's **administration** suffered through **scandals**. But he remained honest and worked hard for the people.

As a young man, Harding bought a struggling newspaper company and made it a success. Then he became a senator and did his best to help people. His hard work paid off when he was elected president of the United States.

President Harding died after less than three years in office. But his ideas and policies were followed by other presidents.

Presidential portrait of Warren G. Harding

Warren G. Harding (1865-1923)
Twenty-ninth President

BORN:	November 2, 1865
PLACE OF BIRTH:	Corsica (Blooming Grove), Ohio
ANCESTRY:	English, Scots-Irish, Dutch
FATHER:	George Tryon Harding (1843-1928)
MOTHER:	Phoebe Dickerson Harding (1843-1910)
WIFE:	Florence Kling DeWolfe (1860-1924)
CHILDREN:	Stepson, Eugene, from wife's first marriage
EDUCATION:	Local schools; Ohio Central College
RELIGION:	Baptist
OCCUPATION:	Newspaper editor and publisher, schoolteacher
MILITARY SERVICE:	None
POLITICAL PARTY:	Republican

OFFICES HELD: Member of Ohio state senate; lieutenant governor of Ohio; U.S. senator

AGE AT INAUGURATION: 55

YEARS SERVED: 1921-1923

VICE PRESIDENT: Calvin Coolidge

DIED: August 2, 1923, San Francisco, California, age 57

CAUSE OF DEATH: Stroke

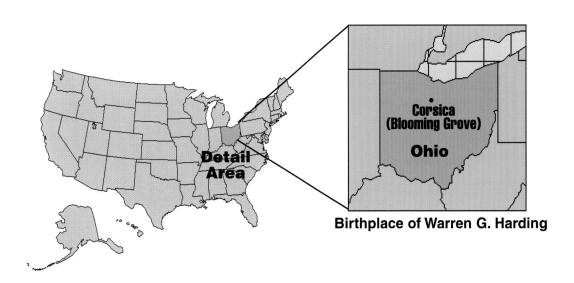

Corsica
(Blooming Grove)

Ohio

Detail Area

Birthplace of Warren G. Harding

Growing Up in Ohio

*W*arren G. Harding was born in Corsica, Ohio, on November 2, 1865. The town is now called Blooming Grove. Warren was the first of eight children born to George and Phoebe Harding.

The Harding family was poor. George supported his family by farming. Warren spent much of his time doing chores. He cut down trees, split rails, chopped wood, and planted and harvested crops.

George bought part ownership in a newspaper. Warren helped any way he could. He liked the newspaper business.

Warren attended a one-room schoolhouse until he was 14 years old. Then he went to Ohio Central College in Iberia, Ohio.

Warren was the editor of the yearbook. He played the cornet, and joined the **debate** team. He graduated in 1882. Then he moved to Marion, Ohio, where his family now lived.

The home of Warren Harding in Marion, Ohio

Harding's First Jobs

*H*arding had many jobs after graduating from Ohio Central. He taught school for one term. He studied to become a lawyer. Then he tried selling insurance.

Harding did not like any of these jobs. Then he remembered how much he liked the newspaper business. He became a reporter for the *Mirror* in Marion.

Harding wrote about community events. He liked political writing most of all. But the *Mirror* was a **Democratic** paper. Harding was a **Republican**.

During the 1884 election, Harding wrote stories supporting the Republican candidate, James G. Blaine. He wore a Blaine campaign hat and button to work. This upset the newspaper owners. They fired Harding.

Another newspaper, the *Marion Star*, was for sale for $300. Harding and two friends bought it.

Warren Harding as a young man

The *Marion Star*

*M*ost people believed Harding was foolish to buy the *Marion Star*. Its building and equipment needed repair. The paper did not have **advertising**. And **subscriptions** cost only 10 cents a week.

Harding worked day and night to make the newspaper successful. He operated the equipment. He wrote articles. And he sold advertising.

Harding got help after he met Florence Kling DeWolfe. She was born in Marion, Ohio, in 1860. Warren and Florence married on July 8, 1891.

Florence began working at the newspaper. Harding trusted his wife's good business sense. Slowly, she took over the business. Now Harding had more time for other interests.

Harding wanted to make his community and state a better place to live. So, he entered politics.

Florence Harding

The Making of the Twenty-ninth United States President

 **1865**

Born November 2, in Corsica, Ohio

 **1875**

Works at his father's newspaper

 **1880**

Enters Ohio Central College in August

 **1884**

Works for the *Mirror*

 **1884**

Buys the *Marion Star*

 **1891**

Marries Florence Kling DeWolfe on July 8

 **1910**

Runs for governor of Ohio but loses

 **1914**

Elected United States senator

 **1917**

United States enters World War I

Warren G. Harding

"I would like to acclaim an era of good feeling amid dependable prosperity and all the blessings which attend."

 **1882**

Graduates from Ohio Central College; teaches school for one term

 **1883**

Studies law; sells insurance

Historic Events
during Harding's Presidency

Peace with Germany and Austria is declared

Insulin first used as a treatment for diabetes

King Tutankhamen's tomb is discovered

 **1898**

Elected to the Ohio State Senate

1902

Elected lieutenant governor of Ohio

1920

Elected president of the United States

1922

Albert Fall leases Teapot Dome to oil companies

1923

Dies August 2, in San Francisco, California

PRESIDENTIAL YEARS

Politics

*H*arding went to town meetings and gave speeches. People liked his ideas. In 1898, Harding was elected to the state senate.

Harding became one of the most popular senators. He was friendly. And he helped keep peace in the **Republican** party. After his re-election, Harding became a party leader. In 1902, he was elected **lieutenant governor** of Ohio.

Harding ran for governor of Ohio in 1910. But he lost the election. Harding's political career seemed over. But in 1912, he gave important speeches at the Republican National **Convention**. He announced President William H. Taft for re-election. And he impressed Republican party leaders with his speaking ability.

Opposite page:
William H. Taft

Senator Harding

*I*n 1914, the **Republicans** chose Harding to run for the U.S. Senate. Harding easily won the election.

Senator Harding voted for two **amendments** to the constitution. One gave women the right to vote. The other stopped the sale of alcohol in America.

During this time, many countries were fighting **World War I**. President Wilson called a special session of **Congress** on April 2, 1917. He wanted the United States to enter the war and help the **Allies** win. Eighty-two senators, including Harding, voted to go to war. Six senators voted no. The United States went to war. The Allies won in November, 1918.

In 1920, Harding wanted to run for senator again. But the Republican party couldn't agree on a choice for president. A group of Republican senators nominated Harding.

The **Republican** party finally chose Harding to run for president. He picked Massachusetts governor Calvin Coolidge to run for vice president.

Governor Calvin Coolidge

President Harding

*T*he U.S. economy suffered in 1920. Businesses lost money. People lost jobs. Americans blamed President Wilson and the **Democrats**.

Harding promised to make the country better. On November 2, 1920, he won the election.

To keep his promise, President Harding helped make new laws. He allowed American businesses to produce more goods. He lowered taxes on U.S. goods. But he raised taxes on goods from other countries. And he slowed **immigration**.

President Harding was working hard and the American people had faith in him. But there were problems with his **administration**. Some people in his **cabinet** were not honest.

President Harding (seated third from right) with his cabinet

The Seven "Hats" of the U.S. President

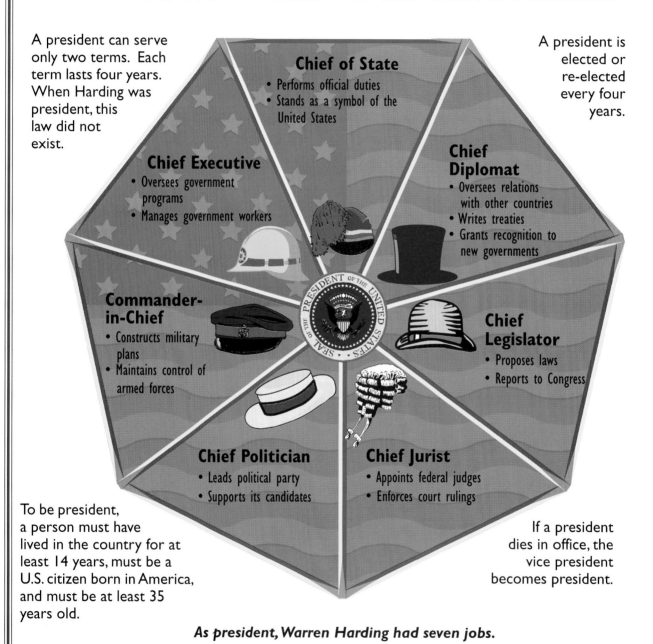

A president can serve only two terms. Each term lasts four years. When Harding was president, this law did not exist.

A president is elected or re-elected every four years.

Chief of State
- Performs official duties
- Stands as a symbol of the United States

Chief Executive
- Oversees government programs
- Manages government workers

Chief Diplomat
- Oversees relations with other countries
- Writes treaties
- Grants recognition to new governments

Commander-in-Chief
- Constructs military plans
- Maintains control of armed forces

Chief Legislator
- Proposes laws
- Reports to Congress

Chief Politician
- Leads political party
- Supports its candidates

Chief Jurist
- Appoints federal judges
- Enforces court rulings

To be president, a person must have lived in the country for at least 14 years, must be a U.S. citizen born in America, and must be at least 35 years old.

If a president dies in office, the vice president becomes president.

As president, Warren Harding had seven jobs.

The Three Branches of the U.S. Government

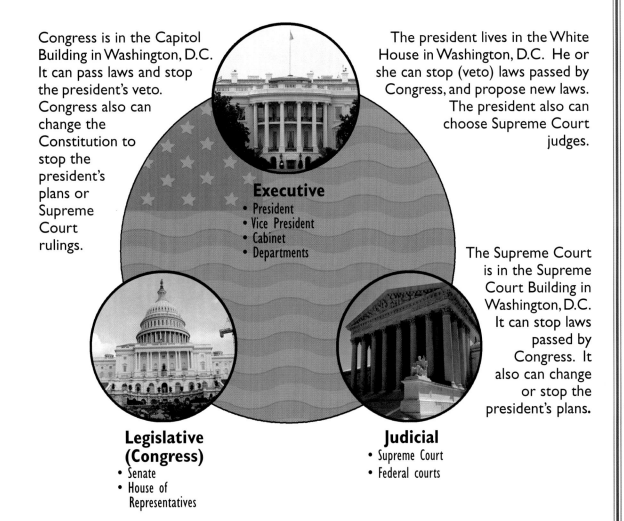

Congress is in the Capitol Building in Washington, D.C. It can pass laws and stop the president's veto. Congress also can change the Constitution to stop the president's plans or Supreme Court rulings.

The president lives in the White House in Washington, D.C. He or she can stop (veto) laws passed by Congress, and propose new laws. The president also can choose Supreme Court judges.

Executive
- President
- Vice President
- Cabinet
- Departments

The Supreme Court is in the Supreme Court Building in Washington, D.C. It can stop laws passed by Congress. It also can change or stop the president's plans.

Legislative (Congress)
- Senate
- House of Representatives

Judicial
- Supreme Court
- Federal courts

The U.S. Constitution formed three government branches. Each branch has power over the others. So, no single group or person can control the country. The Constitution calls this "separation of powers."

Teapot Dome

*A*lbert B. Fall was President Harding's secretary of the interior. He was in charge of America's natural resources. Fall led the Harding **administration** into one of the greatest **scandals** in U.S. history. It was called the Teapot Dome scandal.

Teapot Dome was a piece of government land in Wyoming. Albert Fall allowed oil companies to drill on this land. **Secretary of the Navy** Edwin Denby signed the land agreements. Both men received **bribes** from the oil companies.

Fall went to jail for his crime. Denby was forced to quit. **Congress** also uncovered other crimes in the **Justice Department** and the **Veterans Bureau**.

Opposite page:
Secretary of the Interior
Albert B. Fall

The **scandals** upset President Harding. He had trusted his **cabinet**. Harding and his wife decided to take a trip across the nation and talk to Americans. He wanted to keep their trust.

The trip began in Alaska. Then the Hardings traveled to California. In San Francisco on August 2, 1923, President Harding suffered a stroke and died.

President Harding was buried in Marion in a tomb given by the citizens. Florence moved back to Marion. She died 15 months later. Florence was buried next to her husband.

Warren G. Harding wanted to be America's "best-loved" president. He wanted to restore the war-weary country to a time of "normalcy." But his presidency will always be remembered for the scandals that tarnished his cabinet.

Opposite page:
The funeral of
President Harding

Fun Facts

- Warren G. Harding was the first president to ride in a car to his **inauguration**.

- Harding is the only newspaper publisher to become the president of the United States.

- Warren G. Harding was the first president for whom women could vote.

- Harding was the first president to have a radio in the White House.

- President Harding kept a pen of turkeys at the White House.

- Laddie Boy, President Harding's dog, owned Washington D.C.'s dog license #1. Every day the dog would fetch the president's newspaper.

- Laddie Boy had a birthday party at the White House. A frosted cake made from dog biscuits was served.

- To get in shape for his presidential campaign, Harding played Ping-Pong every morning, tennis every afternoon, and golf three times a week.

- Harding still loved playing the cornet. After college, he decided to form a marching band. He became the manager of the Marion Citizens Cornet Band. The small band won third prize in a state band festival.

- Florence Harding was a popular first lady. When the Hardings moved into the White House, Florence opened the mansion to the public. She put fresh flowers in every room. She opened up the shades, saying, "It's the people's house. If they want to look in, let them." She also held parties at the White House for people who had served in **World War I**.

Glossary

administration - the entire staff who works for a president.

advertising - to announce businesses and events to people.

Allies - countries that agree to help each other in times of need. In World War I, France, Great Britain, and Russia were called the Allies.

amendment - a change to the Constitution of the United States.

bribe - anything given to someone so they will do something wrong.

cabinet - a group of advisers chosen by the president.

Congress - the lawmaking body of the U.S. It is made up of the Senate and the House of Representatives.

convention - a large meeting.

debate - a public talk about topics or questions.

Democrat - one of the two main political parties in the United States. Democrats are often more liberal and believe in more government.

immigration - the movement of people from one country to another.

inauguration - when a person is sworn into office.

Justice Department - the judicial branch of the government.

lieutenant governor - the second highest elected person in a state.

Republican - one of two main political parties in the United States. Republicans are often more conservative and believe in less government.

scandal - an action that brings disgrace or shocks the public.

secretary of the navy - an adviser to the president who helps determine military matters.

subscription - when someone pays money to receive something.

Veterans Bureau - a part of the government that handles veterans matters.

World War I - 1914-1918. The U.S., Great Britain, France, Russia, and their allies fought Germany, Austria-Hungary and their allies.

Internet Sites

Welcome to the White House
www.whitehouse.gov
Visit the official Web site of the White House. There is an introduction from the United States' current president. Also included are extensive biographies of each president, White House history information, art in the White House, first ladies, and first families. Visit the section titled: The White House for Kids, where kids can become more active in the government of the United States.

Presidents of the United States – Potus
www.ipl.org/ref/POTUS/

This excellent Web site has background information and biographies on each president. Also included is election results, cabinet members, presidency highlights, and some fun facts on each of the presidents. Links to historical documents, audio and video files, and other presidential sites are also included to enrich this site.

These sites are subject to change. Go to your favorite search engine and type in United States presidents for more sites.

Pass It On

History enthusiasts: educate readers around the country by passing on information you've learned about presidents or other important people who have changed history. Share your little-known facts and interesting stories. We want to hear from you!

To get posted on the ABDO Publishing Company Web site, email us at "History@abdopub.com"
Visit the ABDO Publishing Company Web site at www.abdopub.com

Index